TO LOVE AND CHERISH

EPHESIANS 5 AND THE CHALLENGE
OF
CHRISTIAN MARRIAGE

ELGIN L. HUSHBECK, JR
with Hannelore Hushbeck

Energion Publications
Gonzalez, Florida
2019

Copyright © 2019, Elgin L. Hushbeck, Jr.
and Hannelore Hushbeck

Scripture taken from the Holy Bible: International Standard
Version®. Copyright © 1996-forever by The ISV Foundation.
ALL RIGHTS RESERVED INTERNATIONALLY.
Used by permission.

Cover Design: Henry E. Neufeld

ISBN: 978-1-63199-708-2

Energion Publications
P. O. Box 841
Gonzalez, FL 32560
energion.com
pubs@energion.com

ACKNOWLEDGMENTS

First and foremost, I want to thank my wife, who has been very patient with me as I have struggled to learn the lessons of this passage over the last four and a half decades. She is my wife, my friend, and my partner. Together, we truly seek to be one. I also want to thank the many students I have had over the years for their input and challenges as they have helped me think through these issues. I want to thank Helen Wisniewski and Kevin & Larissa Munz whose editing and comments, made this a better book. Finally, I want to thank my friends at Energion, my editor Chris Eyre for his valuable suggestions and my publisher Henry Neufeld for his kind support and encouragement.

INTRODUCTION

If you want to strike fear and trembling into their heart, ask a pastor or biblical teacher to speak before a group of women on Ephesians 5:22. This verse is a proof text for many on how the Bible is completely out of touch and archaic. Its teachings are not just to be ignored, but to be actively opposed as patriarchal and oppressive, a dangerous relic of the past. The key offense occurs in the first part of verse 22, with its command, "Wives, submit yourselves to your husbands." Could anything be more at odds with our modern and enlightened view of equality and relationships?

True, for some Christians this is not a troubling verse at all. In fact, for them, it is a proof text for how the world is corrupt and to be rejected for it is destroying the natural, God-given, order of things. I reject this view. Other Christians, however, view it as a prime example of how the Bible is not to be taken literally and without error. As an evangelical Christian believing in the inerrancy of scripture, while I reject the former view, I reject this view as well, and thus I cannot simply ignore this passage as an archaic relic of our patriarchal past.

I would agree Ephesians 5:22 is a particularly challenging verse, but I would also argue it has a lot to teach us, not just concerning the relationship between wives and husbands, but also about issues with translations, how we understand the historical, literary, and biblical context of a passage, and how we apply the meaning of texts to our own lives. It goes to the heart of who we are and how we should relate to one another. It also goes to the heart of the nature of scripture and how God communicates to us, and thus, how we should read and understand the Bible.

To begin to grasp these issues, one only need look at the underlying Greek text behind the command, "Wives, submit yourselves to your husbands." A strictly literal translation of this passage would be "the wives to their own husband." I am not saying the translation is wrong, only that this issue is more complex than it may at first seem, and the passage cannot be correctly understood simply from the passage quoted. This passage has a context, and it cannot be correctly understood apart from that context. This book will be an attempt to understand that context, and in the process what these verses are saying.

The Setting

We will discuss the issues surrounding the historical and biblical contexts as they arise and will start with the literal context. It is easy to see the Bible as discrete units of teaching, digesting them in a piecemeal fashion, because of chapter and verse structure. However, it is important to remember the books of the Bible were not divided up into chapters and verses until the 13th century. While it is true one can understand the book of Proverbs at the verse level and Psalms at the chapter level, most of the books of the Bible were written to be understood as a whole. The book of Ephesians was written as a single letter and should be approached on that basis. There is a reason the material in chapter five occurs at the location it does, before the material in chapter six and after the material in the earlier chapters.

What follows is a brief outline of the letter up to the teaching on marriage. There are several points in this discussion which are disputed by some scholars, such as, did Paul write the letter and was it written to the Ephesians, but I will not attempt to address these or the other issues, nor will I defend my conclusions about them here. These issues are outside the scope of this book and for the most part do not directly concern the teachings on marriage we are discussing. Keep in mind, this is only a brief outline, and I would strongly encourage you to read the entire book of Ephesians and not rely simply on this summary.

The Book of Ephesians is a letter written by Paul to the church in Ephesus. It opens with a mostly standard opening for a first-century letter: *From, To, Greetings*, though as he does in most of his letters, Paul modifies the *Greeting* portion to be statements of grace and peace instead. He would frequently follow this with statements of thanksgiving and prayer, but here, Paul has the second longest sentence in the New Testament, a sentence on God's role in salvation (1:3-14). The sentence emphasizes the Father "chose us in the Messiah before the creation of the world" (1:4), to live for the praise and glory of Christ (1:12) and we "were sealed with the promised Holy Spirit" (1:13). Following this, Paul returns to his normal thanksgiving (1:15-16) and prayer (1:17-19) ending with a magnificent statement on the power of Christ, making clear God has the power to carry out the plan he has made.

Chapter two continues the discussion but changes the focus from God's role in salvation to ours; a role dismally beginning with "You used to be dead." It proceeds to paint a dark picture of the hopelessness of our former state. This all changes beginning in verse four where Paul abandons this dreary line of discussion in mid-sentence with "But God…made us alive." Verses 8-9 summarize this change, "For by such grace you have been saved through faith. This does not come from you; it is the gift of God and not the result of actions, to put a stop to all boasting." Here we begin to get an idea of the reason for the letter: evidently some in Ephesus were boasting of their new status.

Paul continues by contrasting his readers with the Jews (2:11) and how his readers were "excluded from citizenship in Israel" but now they have been brought near (2:13). The picture here is very much a Jewish one, where closeness to God is related to physical closeness to Jerusalem. He then calls for the ending of hostilities and for a peace rooted in Christ, who is "reconciling both groups to God in one body through the cross, on which he eliminated the hostility" (2:16).

It would seem, as in many places, there were Gentile – Jewish tensions in the city of Ephesus, but unlike other locations, here the main problem was with the Gentile believers who saw themselves as superior and the Jews as inferior. This would account for the emphasis on God's role in choosing us before the beginning of creation, and the warning about boasting, along with the calls for peace.

Chapter three starts with "For this reason," a thought Paul will not finish until verse 14, as he goes instead into discussion of the secret of the Gentiles, a secret made known to Paul (3:2) and which we can understand (3:4); a secret that was hidden but was now being revealed (3:5). "This is that secret: The Gentiles are heirs-in-common, members-in-common of the body, and common participants in what was promised by the Messiah Jesus through the gospel" (3:6). Paul was called to proclaim the secret (3:7-9) the church is the union of God's people, the Jews and the Gentiles, and it is through his people God works in the world.

Paul completes the thought he had started in verse 3:1 and again writing, "for this reason" adding "I bow my knee…" and begins his closing prayer for this section (3:14-19) making three requests, that we would be given strength, understanding, and filled with the fullness of God. He closes the first part of the letter with a doxology, the only one to mention the Church.

This teaching about the Church has ramifications as to how we should live, and that is what Paul now focuses on in the second half of the letter. This part of the letter can be divided into five exhortations, each one centered around the concept of how we are to "live" (literally walk), the first one beginning, "I, therefore, the prisoner of the Lord, urge you to live in a way that is worthy of the calling to which you have been called" (4:1).

The first exhortation (4:1-16), and the exhortation that serves as a foundation for all the rest, is a call for unity. The second (4:17-32) is a negative exhortation not to live as the Gentiles do. The third exhortation (5:1-5) is to live in Love, while the fourth (5:6-14) is a call to live in the light.

This brings us to the exhortation that contains the teaching on marriage. Building on the earlier part of the letter, this exhortation starts, "So, then, be careful how you live. Do not be unwise but wise." (5:15) The main part of the exhortation starts with a long sentence beginning with the dual commands to "Stop getting drunk with wine, which leads to wild living, but keep on being filled with the Spirit" (5:18) which is then followed by a series of participles describing the results of being filled with the Spirit.

In most translations, this long sentence is broken up primarily to avoid long sentences in English, and the participles changed to regular verbs to make the sentences complete. Thus in the translation quoted in this book, the International Standard Version (ISV), the participle for "reciting" is translated as "Then you will recite"; "singing and making music" becomes "you will sing and make music"; while "giving thanks" becomes "you will give thanks"

5

(5:19-20). Normally this does not cause any problems, but it does, at times, make what was a result seem to be a command, as when "singing and making music" is translated as "Sing and make music." This brings us to the text on which we will be focusing.

EPHESIANS 5:21-33

Submitting one to another (5:21)

5:21   and you will submit to one another out of reverence for the Messiah.

The first verse of the section on marriage is transitional, linking the statements on being filled with the Holy Spirit to the discussion on wives and husbands that follows. The phrase "and you will submit to one another out of reverence for the Messiah" in the ISV follows that same translational pattern of the previous verses with the participle "submitting" being translated as "and you will submit." As such, "submitting to one another" is another result of being filled by the Holy Spirit, just like reciting, singing, making music, and giving thanks.

While this verse is the last of the series of verses on being filled with the Holy Spirit, two factors show this is also an integral part of the passage on wives and husbands. The first is that this verse provides the context, and more importantly the verb, for the next verse. The next verse does not make any sense without this one. As we mentioned earlier, a strictly literal translation of 5:22 says, "the wives to their own husband." To their own husbands what? It is only when read along with the previous verse does it make any sense. Translated literally, this reads, "…submitting to one another in reverence for the Messiah, wives to their own husbands…"

The second factor showing this verse is part of the teaching on marriage is this verse is the first part of a two-part rhetorical device used to mark off a section of text. At the time of this letter, writing was in all capital letters with no spaces, punctuation, paragraphs, section headers or other means of formatting texts. Thus, writers had to rely on rhetorical devices for such purposes, which is not merely an ancient practice. While you may not have noticed them, movies and television shows still employ some of these same devices.

The particular rhetorical device here is called an *inclusio*; it is used to mark off a section. You can think of an inclusio as book-ends, such as a movie beginning and ending in the same place to give a sense of completion. You can see this in movies such as the classic Citizen Kane' beginning and ending with Rosebud, or the television series "Star Trek: The Next Generation," where the very last episode of the series involved locations and events, which happened in the pilot episode.

In the section we are presently reviewing, the passage is marked off by calls for reverence at the beginning (v21) and ending (v33). As the transitional verse, verse 21 is both the culmination of the previous section and the backdrop for the teaching on marriage which follows. Consequently, understanding this verse is key to understanding the passage as a whole.

This verse contains two parts, what we should be doing (submitting to one another) and why we should be doing it (reverence for the Messiah). The Greek word translated *submitting* (ὑποτασσόμενοι) is grammatically called a middle-passive participle, and here it indicates a voluntary submission or the voluntary placing oneself under the control of another. It is not an imperative (i.e., a command), which means it is something one chooses to do. It cannot be demanded, coerced, or forced and still be within the discussion here.

The idea of submitting to one another is perfectly in line with the letter up to this point and makes good sense within the context of the letter. We have seen injunctions against boasting (2:10), along with calls for reconciliation and an end to hostilities (2:26). The second half of the letter begins with a call for unity (4:4-16), while other sections speak of an end to quarreling (4:31), and instead call us to be forgiving (4:32). In many ways, the teaching here is very similar to Paul's teaching in Philippians 2:1-4,

> Therefore, if there is any comfort in the Messiah, if there is any consolation of love, if there is any participation in the Spirit, if there is any compassion and

7

sympathy, ₂then fill me with joy by having the same attitude, sharing the same love, being united in spirit, and keeping one purpose in mind. ₃Do not act out of selfish ambition or conceit, but with humility think of others as being better than yourselves. ₄Do not be concerned about your own interests, but also be concerned about the interests of others.

Again, these are not things to be commanded, but things that flow from being filled with the Holy Spirit (v18). This brings us to an important concept in understanding the Bible as a whole, which is that, for the most part, we should read the Bible as primarily written to us to apply in our own lives, not for us to demand others apply in their lives. This is the main idea behind Jesus statement in Matthew 7,

> "Stop judging, so that you won't be judged, ₂because the way that you judge others will be the way that you will be judged, and you will be evaluated by the standard with which you evaluate others. ₃"Why do you see the speck in your brother's eye but fail to notice the beam in your own eye? ₄Or how can you say to your brother, 'Let me take the speck out of your eye,' when the beam is in your own eye? ₅You hypocrite! First remove the beam from your own eye, and then you will see clearly enough to remove the speck from your brother's eye." (Matthew 7:1-5)

A quick way to end up in trouble is to see the Bible as primarily discussing what others should be doing. Nowhere is this more important than here. See Ephesians 5 as primarily important for your spouse and disaster will almost inevitably follow.

It is also important to point out that there is no sense of superiority/inferiority implied here, not even a hint. Luke 2:51 states Jesus was in submission to his parents, yet, as God, he was hardly inferior to them. Still he submitted to them. In addition, rather than being inferior, the equality of all believers, including men and women, is directly stated by Paul in Galatians 3:28, "Because all of you are one in the Messiah Jesus, a person is no longer a Jew or a Greek, a slave or a free person, a male or a female."

If it is not because they are inferior, then why should anyone submit? The second part of 5:21 gives the reason, which is "out of reverence for the Messiah." The word translated *reverence* here is the Greek word *phobos* (φόβος) and is particularly troublesome in this context. Basically, the word means fear, but for many people this conjures up images of a small child cowering before a Dickensian schoolmaster, threatening to beat them. This is not at all what is portrayed in this passage.

As a result, many modern translations translate this as *reverence*, but whereas fear, with its negative connotations, is probably too strong, reverence is probably too weak. The reference here is an understanding and respect for who Jesus is and what he has done for us. It is not a concept of having to walk on eggshells lest we upset him, but rather an understanding he loves us and died for our sins. It is his actions that saved us and allows us to be in a relationship with God. Our relationship with God is not to be taken lightly or haphazardly but with serious concern and an understanding of what it would be like without him.

The main point here is that as we submit to one another we should all be in submission to Jesus. The concept of mutual submission out of the fear/reverence of Jesus is key. Get this right, and the teaching that follows will fall into place. Without it, what follows will be impossible. Still, there is one more issue concerning the submission referred to here, and that is whether the submission is completely mutual or whether it is within an ordered structure.

Ideally, this would be completely mutual, as is described in the Philippians passage cited above, and it is tempting to say it is the focus here. In that case, we would see "submitting to one another" in the same way as "accepting one another in love" was used in 4:2. The problem with this view is that while the Bible teaches us how things should be, it frequently deals with us where we currently are.

Perhaps the clearest example of this is with Jesus' teaching on the nature of marriage and the issue of divorce in Matthew 19:1-12. There He lays out the idea,

"Haven't you read that the one who made them at the beginning 'made them male and female' $_5$and said, 'That is why a man will leave his father and mother and be united with his wife, and the two will become one flesh'? $_6$So they are no longer two, but one flesh. Therefore, what God has joined together, man must never separate." (Matthew 19:5-6)

Asking Jesus why Moses had allowed for divorce if this is the case, He replied, "It was because of your hardness of heart that Moses allowed you to divorce your wives. But from the beginning it was not this way." (Matthew 19:8) The ideal case is there would be no divorce, but it is clear we do not always live up to the ideal and so God deals with us where we are.

This is a huge problem for some. For example, following the teaching on wives and husbands and then parents and children there is a section on slaves and masters. Some see this as an acceptance of slavery where there should instead be a condemnation. This acceptance of slavery is for some another reason to discard the Bible as morally defective.

What would have been the impact of such a condemnation, if God had just condemned slavery instead? Given how often God's laws were ignored, any condemnation of slavery would likely have been ignored as well. Yet, as many governments have found, at times, the regulation of something undesirable is often far more effective than a complete ban.

Slavery was rooted very deeply into the fabric of society for most of history. Any outright ban would likely have had as much impact as an attempt to get rid of currency and return to a barter system would today. In place of an outright ban, the Bible sought instead to regulate slavery. The wisdom of God's approach is seen in Jewish culture.

The Old Testament discourages slavery. After all, the key story of the Hebrew Bible, the Exodus, is the story of being freed from slavery. Despite this, the Old Testament does allow for slavery and calls for a humane treatment rather than an outright ban. As a result of the rules on slavery, over time a saying developed among the Jews that, "anyone who acquires a Hebrew slave acquires a master for himself" (Talmud - Mas. Kiddushin 20a).

It is true the Bible did allow slavery, but also planted the seeds leading those cultures that were strongly influenced by the Bible to treat slaves humanely, greatly reduce slavery, and eventually abolish it. The abolitionist movements were at their core grounded in Judeo-Christian teachings, rooted in the Bible.

Given that at times God speaks to us where we are, and not always where we should be, it is far more likely that what is being referred to in the phrase "submitting to one another" (4:21) is an ordered submission. Whatever the ideal may be, the society of the 1st century was an ordered hierarchal structure where, with the possible exception of Caesar, everyone had to submit to someone at some point. As such, "submitting to one another" in this verse should be understood within this historical framework: Submit to the people to whom you should be submitting.

God's allowance of something is not to say this is how it was and thus how it always should be. Making a claim, as some did, that slavery was in the Bible and therefore was ordained by God, is false. It would be like saying divorce is in the Bible, so there is no big deal pursuing a divorce. In speaking to us where we are, God uses human conventions, and it is important to remember he is not locking in a ceiling but setting a floor. The Bible is not saying don't do it any better, but instead, don't get any worse.

Given all this, the submission here is most likely ordered within the societal framework of the time. Some take this as meaning that, as this discussion moves to the particular instance of wives and husband, we are in the structured section and should focus on the "submitting" part and can effectively ignore the "one another" part, but this does not do justice to the context and setting. Together "submitting" and "one another" are important to understanding what follows.

Wives and Husbands (5:22-33)

The literary structure of the teaching about wives and the teaching about husbands is very carefully written to link this teaching into what has already come before and to each other. Earlier I

11

mentioned this passage is marked off with an inclusio in verses 21 and 33. The internal structure of this section uses another rhetorical device several times. The device used here is called a *chiasmus*, which is used to highlight points and provide emphasis. Named after the Greek letter *chi* (X), a chiasmus refers to a literary structure where the discussion begins at one point, and then with particular words, phrases, or concepts move progressively towards the center point, and then back out in reverse order to the beginning point. Broken apart and structured to make the chiasmus easily visible, the points leading to the center are labeled A; B; C; etc., while the corresponding points leading away from the center are labeled C'; B'; and A'. An example of a small chiasmus is John F Kennedy's statement, "Ask not what your country can do for you, but what you can do for your country." This has the pattern:

A – country
    B – you
    B' – you
A'– country.

Notice how this naturally emphasizes the center, in this case, you. You do not need to know this is a chiasmus to understand this. When it comes to the Bible, because of the issues of translation, these are not always as apparent and often literary features are lost. Still understanding this structure can help us see the emphasis where the author intended it to be.

The teaching on wives and husbands is particularly complex because it is not just a chiasmus, it is a large chiasmus also containing two smaller ones. It can be organized as follows:

A   v22
    B   v23-24 – smaller Chiasmus
        C   v25
            D   v26
                E   v27a
            D'   v27b
        C' v28a
    B' v28b-33a – smaller Chiasmus
A' v33b

The result is a very complex passage with a lot going on, particularly when you consider that the teaching about marriage is tied closely to the teaching of the Church which Paul has spent a good portion of the letter discussing. In verse 32 he describes this as "a great secret." This complexity should not be surprising. Experience has shown that marriage is not easy. There are a lot of moving parts, things to factor in, in order to get it right. Having a good marriage takes a lot of work on both sides, but when it works, the benefits are tremendous.

5:22 Wives, submit yourselves to your husbands as to the Lord.

A – paired with A' in v33b

Paul starts by taking the established norms for his time, and without actually rejecting them, he turns them on their head. While I argued above for an understanding against a backdrop of first-century society, Paul does not completely conform to first-century norms but instead is pushing the boundaries. While two thousand years later it may not be readily apparent, the contrast begins with the first word, "wives."

Marriage at the time was strongly influenced by Greco-Roman culture, which, at least initially, saw the husband as sort of a king. As Aristotle put it, "government controls men who are by nature free, the master's authority men who are by nature slaves; and the government of a household is monarchy (since every house is governed by a single ruler)" (Aristotle *Politics* 1255b).

Now it is true, by the first century, the position of some women was improving somewhat in Rome. Traditionally, the legal rights of a woman would be transferred from the father to the husband, but by the first century often this did not happen, effectively leaving Roman women with more rights than in the past, though still not seen as equal in a modern sense and the husband ruled the family. Household codes from this era can be summed up as instructions for men to rule their families well.

Against this backdrop, Paul breaks with this tradition in three ways. The first is that he addresses the wives at all. Normally such instructions were addressed, not to wives, but only to husbands who were instructed to keep their wives under control. Secondly, making matters worse, at least from the perspective of the time, he addresses them first. Again, this is difficult to appreciate two thousand years later, but at the time Paul wrote, wives would not normally be addressed at all, and if addressed, it would only be after the husband. In addressing the wives directly and first, Paul turns the cultural order and conventions upside down. More importantly, he addresses them as moral equals whom he is trying to encourage and persuade, not as inferior people to be ordered around. (Note: Paul does the same thing with children, and slaves in the two sections following this.)

Another distinction in the passage, in contrast with the ancient household codes, is in the choice of words. The ancient codes normally speak of obedience, and in fact, in the following section children are told to obey their parents. Here, the concept is not of obedience but voluntary submission. The distinction may at first seem minor. It is true at times these terms are used interchangeably. It is also true there is a huge difference between voluntary submission, which can only be given, and forced obedience, which is demanded, particularly here in the context of addressing a moral equal, one choosing to submit, just as we all submit one to another.

One could object, as many have, why must it be the wife who submits? Why not the husband? This is a fair question, but as we will see shortly, ultimately an irrelevant one, so I will postpone that discussion for later.

Many problems arise if the discussion starts and ends with the first part of this verse. However, I would argue the second part, "as to the Lord" is just as important, if not more so, for this explains what is being discussed. The way in which wives are to submit to their husbands is the same way they submit to the Lord. This raises the fundamental question of why do we submit to Jesus?

For some, particularly non-Christians without a good knowledge of the teaching of the New Testament, we submit because it is something we must do to earn salvation. The first half of the letter dispels any such notion. As noted above the letter opens with a very clear statement that those who are saved were chosen "in the Messiah before the creation of the world" (1:4). In chapter two, Paul further explains, "For by such grace you have been saved

14

through faith. This does not come from you; it is the gift of God and not the result of actions, to put a stop to all boasting" (2:8-9).

Elsewhere, Paul describes the futility of attempting to please God by works: "do not misapply God's grace, for if righteousness comes about by doing what the Law requires, then the Messiah died for nothing" (Galatians 2:21). Any attempt to earn God's favor by doing good works is doomed for "all have sinned and continue to fall short of God's glory" (Romans 3:23). Why should Christians do good works, if this is the case?

The answer is seen in Christ's reinstatement of Peter. Three times Peter denied Christ, so Jesus asked Peter three times, "Do you love me?" Each time after Peter replied he did, Jesus responded: "Feed my sheep" (John 21:15-17). We submit to Jesus, not to earn salvation, which is a gift of God that cannot be earned, only accepted, we submit to God, voluntarily out of love. Likewise, the wife submits, not out of any sense of duty or obligation, but out of love.

5:23-24 For the husband is the head of his wife as the Messiah is the head of the church. It is he who is the Savior of the body. ₂₄Indeed, just as the church is submissive to the Messiah, so wives must be submissive to their husbands in everything.

B – paired with B' in v28b-33a

The next two verses are an expansion on the previous verse and make up the first of the two smaller chiasmi embedded in the large chiasmus of this section, with the other chiasmus, as expected being found in the corresponding passage B' (v28b-33a). Note how this passage goes husband, wife, Christ, Church, with the center on Savior; and then in reverse order Church, Christ, wife, husband. Laid out to make the Chiasmus more visible, it reads as follows:

a – For the husband is the head
  b – of the wife
    c – as the Messiah is the head
      d – of the church.
        e – It is he who is the Savior of the body.
      d' – But as the church
    c' – is submissive to the Messiah,
  b' – so wives also
a' – to their husbands in everything.

This section begins with a purpose/explanation clause (For) and then proceeds to explain the submission with a metaphor comparing a husband's and wife's relationship in marriage to the Church's relationship with Christ. What is unique here is that this reverses the normal metaphor, which compares the Church's relationship with Christ to marriage. Immediately two issues come up when trying to understand this passage.

The first is in trying to understand how the Christ/Church relationship is a metaphor for marriage. As I am sure most wives would be quick to point out, their husbands are not Christ, and they are not the church. In all metaphors, there is always an issue as to how far they can be pressed before they break down. As such, it is best to stick to the main points stated by the person making the metaphor, as straying too far from those is always risky.

The second issue is trying to understand the usage of the word "head." Before we can understand how the husband is the head of the wife, we must first understand how Christ is the head of the Church. It does not help that earlier in the letter, Paul used the same word translated "head" with different connotations. In the early part of the letter, he wrote that,

> God has put everything under the Messiah's feet
> and has made him the head of everything for the good
> of the church, which is his body, the fullness of the one
> who fills everything in every way. (1:22-23)

This has a clear implication of governing or ruling. Later in the letter, Paul again references Christ as the head but with a different meaning,

> Instead, by speaking the truth in love, we will grow
> up completely and become one with the head, that is,
> one with the Messiah, in whom the whole body is unit-
> ed and held together by every ligament with which it is
> supplied. As each individual part does its job, the body
> builds itself up in love. (4:15-16)

Here the reference is not to governing but more as a source that feeds, nourishes, and supports, more like 'head' in the head waters of a river refers to the source of the river.

So as Paul uses the word "head" in relation to Christ and the Church in Ephesians, there are two different meanings: one is to rule or govern, the other is to support, supply, or build up. Deciding between the two understandings is not easy. In the smaller chiasmus, the corresponding passage (c') says, "is submissive to the Messiah," which could point to it having the meaning of governing. On the other hand, the two earlier references to head that used the meaning of source, were both closer and more directly applied to the Church, than the use as to rule at the beginning of the book.

One problem with head being a reference to governing is that it results in this passage being a pattern, not a reason: Jesus is the bridegroom and the head of the church; therefore, the husband is the head of the family. Given the inherent equality of both husband and wife, and that someone has to be the head, perhaps it is as simple as this, but if so, it is not very satisfying if taken as a reason, for this would easily breakdown into a tautology or circular reasoning. The husband is the head because the head is the husband. In addition, the context here, starting with "for" would seem to indicate a reason rather than a pattern.

Given this, and the earlier references to Jesus as the head of the church indicating a source or support, it would seem better to take this here as a source. At the time Paul wrote, this was the cultural norm; wives did depend on their husbands, at least within the bounds of the metaphor the Church depends on Christ. This understanding would also line up very well with the center of the Chiasmus, "It is he who is the Savior of the body," which is much closer to a statement of the source (i.e., the one who provides salvation) rather than of governance (i.e., the one who rules).

17

Having laid out this justification for submission, the passage unwinds the chiasmus predictably, starting with the submission of the church as a picture for the wife. However, once again Paul avoids using the word in relation to wives, instead simply saying "so wives also." It is as if he is trying to ensure these statements are not taken out of context. By writing "wives to their own husbands" and "so wives also" he is attempting to force consideration of the overall context.

At a macro level, Paul sticks with the cultural norms for the society in which he lived. Wives are to be subject to their husbands, but he does so by blowing up the foundations supporting them: the inferiority of women, and the natural right of the man to rule. He instead writes to women as equals and provides Christian reasons based on the metaphor of the church.

If this understanding is correct, then it has some interesting implications when applied to a social context that is markedly different from that to which Paul was addressing. Would this mean that given a situation where the wife was in the role as the "source" for the husband, as in the case of a working mother, with a stay-at-home dad, should she then likewise be the head? I do not see any reason why not. Of course, Paul did not address this question, and, at this point, he turns his attention to the other half of the marriage equation. Again, he breaks with the norms of his day.

5:25 Husbands, love your wives as the Messiah loved the church and gave himself for it.

C – paired with C' in v28a

Since he had already broken with convention by addressing the wives, and addressing them first, his addressing husband second is likewise a break with convention. However, he does more than just that, for he begins with the command "Husbands, love your wives." This is a break with his own convention within this section for it is the first imperative (command) since verse 18, where he started with the command "be filled with the Holy Spirit." What has followed since is a series of participles detailing the results of being filled ending with "submitting to one another" in verse 21 and then the instructions to wives.

While the major Greek texts insert a period after verse 21 (ancient manuscript contain no punctuation), a good case can be made the sentence actually ends after the initial instructions to women as there is no main verb in that passage. As pointed out before, all it says is, "wives to their own husbands" and the verb comes from the previous statement about "submitting to one another." As we saw, Paul avoids using submitting and women together, requiring the reader to infer it from the context. Not only is there no such inference required here this is written as an imperative, a direct command, "Husbands, love your wives."

There is another break with the conventions of the times, one not as readily apparent to readers two thousand years later, the mention of love. In the Greek and Roman household codes of the era, love plays no role and is not mentioned. A Roman reading this passage might easily have asked, foreseeing a modern song, "What's Love got to do with it?" Even in Jewish household codes love is only rarely mentioned. An ancient Roman reader would have expected a discussion more along the lines of how the husband was to rule over their household or how they were to keep their family under their control. Yet, even though the section written to husbands is three-times longer than the section written to women (143 words, to 47 words), there is nothing in here about ordering, controlling, or ruling.

Thus, Paul continues to disrupt the norm, but he is not just disrupting first-century norms but also challenging modern conventions as well. One of the key tenets of modern culture is the uncontrollability of love. Numerous movies and novels are grounded in the uncontrollability of love. For many TV shows, you are either in love or you are not, and there is not much you can do about it. Love is portrayed as just something that happens. Many excuses for things like adultery are based on following your heart, which is frequently portrayed by modern culture as not just an option, but a noble calling, if not the highest calling.

In contrast, the consistent message of the Bible is that love is something you can control. Earlier in the letter we are commanded to "love one another" (4:2). Jesus tells us to love our neighbor (Mark 12:31) and Leviticus 19:34 says of the stranger that we should "love him like yourself." Throughout the Bible, love is consistently portrayed as a choice, not an uncontrollable impulse, and lack of love is never an excuse.

Husbands are not commanded to rule, but to love and the example husbands are to follow is that of Jesus' love for the church; a very tall order made even more so by the example given as Jesus "gave himself for it." This is not a call for husbands to be the heroic savior, sacrificing their life in some life-threatening situation; that would be too easy. Instead, this is a call for how husbands are to live their day to day lives.

While a new command and a new sentence, it is important to remember this is still within the inclusio marking off verse 21-33 and thus within the section described by "submitting to one another." In love, there is a form of submitting. While Jesus is the head, his leadership of the church is not defined by being the boss and giving orders, but by being a servant, a style of leadership recently come to be called servant leadership.

While servant leadership almost seems like an oxymoron; it is a style of leadership putting the needs of others before yourself. Your actions as a leader are centered on serving others, not what is best for you. A good example of Servant leadership is the following account from the night of the last supper,

> Now before the Passover Festival, Jesus realized that his hour had come to leave this world and return to the Father. Having loved his own who were in the world, he loved them to the end. By supper time, the devil had already put it into the heart of Judas, the son of Simon Iscariot, to betray him. Because Jesus knew that the Father had given everything into his control, that he had come from God, and that he was returning to God. Therefore he got up from the table, removed his outer robe, and took a towel and fastened it around his waist. Then he poured some water into a basin and began to wash the disciples' feet and to dry them with the towel that was tied around his waist. (John 13:1-5)

Washing the feet of a guest was a task assigned to the lowest slave. As such, to a more traditional leader, this does not make sense. By the conventions of the time, Jesus was the last person who should have done this. Something Peter recognized when he objected "You must never wash my feet!" (John 13:8) Still, Jesus did it, not in spite of his being a leader, but because he was. "Because Jesus knew that the Father had given everything into his control, that he had come from God, and that he was returning to God, therefore..." (John 13:3).

In a more traditional leadership style, Jesus would have just ordered his disciple to do what he wanted, but instead of doing this Jesus was leading by example: "if I, your Lord and Teacher, have washed your feet, you must also wash one another's feet. I've set an example for you, so that you may do as I have done to you" (John 13:14-15). Nor was this simply a call to wash feet, it was a call on how to be a leader; to lead by service and sacrifice for the good of others.

Peter learned from this example and passed it on to those he taught,

> Therefore, as a fellow elder, a witness of the Mes-
> siah's sufferings, and one who shares in the glory to be
> revealed, I appeal to the elders among you: Be shepherds
> of God's flock that is among you, watching over it, not
> because you must but because you want to, and not
> greedily but eagerly, as God desires. Do not lord it over
> the people entrusted to you, but be examples to the
> flock. (1 Peter 5:1-3)

This is the type of leader Paul is calling husbands to be; leaders who lead by service and sacrifice for the good of their wives, not to be the boss, but the servant.

5:26 so that he might make it holy by cleansing it, washing it with water and the word

D – paired with D' in v27b

This command for husbands to love their wives based on the example of Christ is followed by three purpose clauses, (D, E, D') giving the reason or purpose for his love and his servant leadership. This passage is a very difficult part to understand, which is something Paul, himself, will point out shortly, for it is talking about Christ's love for the Church as a metaphor for a husband's love for his wife. As with all metaphors, there is always a difficulty in determining how literally to take the metaphor, and how far the metaphor extends. As such, I will attempt to stick only the main points, and not stray too far from them, and will point out what I think are some possible errors.

The first purpose clause gives as a reason "so that he might make it holy." As was made clear in the first half of the letter, salvation is an act of God's choice, and not our being worthy. "For by such grace you have been saved through faith. This does not come from you; it is the gift of God and not the result of actions, to put a stop to all boasting" (2:8-9). God did not choose the church because the church was holy, he chose the church to make it holy.

This was accomplished "by cleansing it, washing it with water and the word," which is a picture of salvation, Baptism, and the Gospel. It is a reference to how Christ saved us, not by demanding we conform to his will, but as an act of grace grounded in love, his sacrificial death on the cross. He completely gave himself to us.

The main lesson for husbands is their love and sacrifice is not conditional. There can be no valid excuses beginning "Well if she would just…." Contrast this with "But God demonstrates his love for us by the fact that the Messiah died for us while we were still sinners" (Romans 5:8). In short, the focus here is on Christ and what he did, and by inference the husband, not the wife.

5:27a and might present the church to himself in all its glory, without a spot or wrinkle or anything of the kind

E – Center of Chiasmus

The second of the three purpose clauses is also the center of the larger chiasmus, and thus can be seen as the central point of the teaching to wives and husbands as a whole. Thus, it is not a coincidence this is also the main goal of the metaphor, and by inference of marriage. The reason for Christ's sacrificial love is to present the church to him as his bride. It is the perfect love leading to the perfect result, the perfect bride in the perfect marriage, the union of Christ and the Church.

By inference, this is also the reason for the husband's sacrificial love; husband and wife can come together in the perfect marriage. In many respects, it is a goal that can never be achieved, but the closer a couple gets, the better their relationship and thus their marriage will be.

5:27b   but holy and without fault.

D' – paired with D in v26

Having reached the center of the chiasmus, Paul now works his way back out with corresponding statements to those leading up to the center. In a chiasmus, the parallels passages can be reinforcing, contrasting, or simply linked by similar wording or grammar. Here they are reinforcing. Thus, v 26 which stated, "so that he might make it holy by cleansing it, washing it with water and the word," is reinforced with "but holy and without fault." The perfection of the Church is a goal of sacrificial love, not a condition for it. Likewise, the perfection of the marriage is a goal, not a condition.

5:28a   In the same way, husbands must love their wives as they love their own bodies

C' – paired with C in v25

Paul now returns to his initial command for husbands to love their wives. In the parallel passage of the chiasmus, husbands were to "love your wives as the Messiah loved the church and gave himself for it," which led him into the central part of the chiasmus and the perfect union of Jesus and the Church. So there is no confusion, Paul now makes explicit what he has just said about Christ and the Church, applies to husbands, "In the same way…" Here, however, the command is expressed slightly differently. "Husbands must love their wives as they love their own bodies."

The basic instruction to wives at the beginning of the Chiasmus (A) was expanded/explained by a smaller chiasmus (B). So, it should not be surprising having now repeated the basic instruction for husbands, this will likewise be expanded/explained in the next section (B') with another small chiasmus.

5:28b - 5:33a A man who loves his wife loves himself. For no one has ever hated his own body, but he nourishes and tenderly cares for it, as the Messiah does the church. For we are parts of his body—of his flesh and of his bones. "That is why a man will leave his father and mother and be united with his wife, and the two will become one flesh." This is a great secret, but I am talking about the Messiah and the church. But each individual man among you must love his wife as he loves himself;

B' – paired with B in v23-24

Given the amount of text devoted to men is three times longer than that devoted to women, it is not surprising this chiasmus is larger than the corresponding chiasmus in B. It is not larger just because Paul is addressing husbands, but as he is coming to the end of the section, Paul is bringing together several of the themes of this very difficult teaching. Here is the text laid out to make the chiasmus easier to see.

a – A man who loves his wife loves himself. For no one has ever hated his own body, but he nourishes and tenderly cares for it,

b – as the Messiah does the church.

c – For we are parts of his body— of his flesh and of his bones.

d – "That is why a man will leave his father and mother and be united with his wife, and the two will become one flesh."

c' – This is a great secret,

b' – but I am talking about the Messiah and the church.

a' – But each individual man among you must love his wife as he loves himself;

Paul begins by expanding on what he has just said. "A man who loves his wife loves himself." The importance of this point is made clear by the fact, Paul then expands on it. "For no one has ever hated his own body, but he nourishes and tenderly cares for it." In terms of style, this second part is unnecessary for the chiastic

24

structure, as the first part "A man who loves his wife loves himself" matches very well with the closing part of the chiasmus "But each individual man among you must love his wife as he loves himself." It is there for emphasis.

This is a very important point for Paul, one he does not want his readers to miss. Given the backdrop of the era, this is not surprising, for his point runs counter to the common view of the period. The division between men and women was a given, based on the supposed inferiority of the women. Force and power dominated. Rome ruled because it was strong. Slaves were slaves because they were weak. It was seen as the natural order of things. Thus women, as physically weaker than men, were inferior, and it was just their nature to be ruled. In contrast to this view, Paul does not say women should be ruled, but loved, and not just loved, but loved as the husband loves himself.

Paul drives home his point here both negatively, "for no one has ever hated his own body," and positively "but he nourishes and tenderly cares for it," which is another means of emphasis. A wife is not a servant to order about, but an equal to be loved. After all, how successful would it be to order your body to lose weight or get stronger? Marriage is a relationship that involves nurturing and caring.

From here Paul again returns to the example of Christ and the church. Throughout this passage, two things are going on, Paul is teaching about husbands and wives, and also teaching about Christ and the Church, each mirroring the other.

There is a sudden change in verse 30 as Paul makes this very personal. Until now he has been taking in 3rd person, about husbands, wives, Christ, and the church, but here he suddenly changes to the first person "we." "For we are parts of his body—of his flesh and of his bones." The teaching here is much more than a simple household code about the conduct of husbands and wives.

Here Paul is drawing upon his teachings earlier in Ephesians. Much of the letter has been about God's plan for the Church, the building up of the church and its work in the world. 1:22-23 states "for the good of the church, which is his body." Verse 4:12 states the offices and roles within the church were "to build up the body of the Messiah." Now with the picture of a husband's love for his wife as himself, Paul says we are part of the body of Christ.

He then cites Genesis 2:24 as support, "That is why a man will leave his father and mother and be united with his wife, and the two will become one flesh." In terms of the Chiasmus this is the center and thus the focus of the reason, "husbands must love their wives as they love their own bodies." He is using the picture of the marriage of Christ and the church as his guide. We will become one with Jesus.

Paul admits, "This is a great secret." There is some discussion about whether the Greek word here should be translated mystery (something difficult to figure out) or secret (something hidden, but possibly now revealed). Either way, there are aspects of this that are difficult to understand. 'Great' refers to profound/important, rather than difficult/deep. Not only is the Genesis quote emphasized by it being the center of the Chiasmus, Paul directly states its importance.

The statement "but I am talking about the Messiah and the church" picks up the parallel passage of the chiasmus and reminds the reader that these passages refer to the church. This secret is Christ's work which is revealed in the church. Paul closes the chiasmus where he started, "But each individual man among you must love his wife as he loves himself."

The importance of the command for husbands to love their wives is seen in the fact it is repeated three times (v 25, 28a, 33) and is explained by using Christ's love for the Church. Husbands are to love their wives as themselves in light of the citation of Genesis 2:24 so that, "the two will become one flesh" was in stark contrast to the household codes of the era.

Loving someone as yourself implies inherent equality. What could be more equal to you than you? Something cannot be lesser and equal at the same time; it cannot be yourself and lesser than yourself at the same time. It is likewise true with the concept of the two becoming one, if the two become one, they cannot also be unequal.

This is why the question mentioned earlier as to why it is the wife, and not the husband, that must submit is ultimately irrelevant. Seeing wives as submitting to their husband was the cultural norm asking nothing more than what was already expected by society. Calling on husbands to have sacrificial love for their wives, seeing them as equals and one with them, was a radical break. He called on husbands to follow the example of Christ. So while Paul starts with the ordered structure of his day, his teaching ultimately undermines it calling for equality of union, making perfect sense of the verse that started this section, "and you will submit to one another out of reverence for the Messiah." (v21).

5:33b   and may the wife fear her husband

A' – paired with A in v22

Paul now closes out the chiasmus where he began, with the wife. He is also marking the end of the section with an inclusio with verse 21. The use of fear here in this verse has all the same issues as it did in verse 21, where we pointed out the difficulty of translating the Greek word into English. Given the inclusio, the comparison to the church is easy to see wives are to view their husbands the same way the church views Jesus, with love.

PUTTING IT ALL TOGETHER

A theme within the letter up to this point has been harmony and unity. 2:14 said of Jesus "For it is he who is our peace. Through his mortality he made both groups one by tearing down the wall of hostility that divided them." In verse 4:2 "Do your best to maintain the unity of the Spirit by means of the bond of peace." He tells us to "be kind to one another, compassionate, forgiving one another just as God has forgiven you in the Messiah" (4:32). So, it should not be a surprise to see him include a form of household codes to bring harmony to the family.

Yet Paul's household code is not a traditional first-century household code. While seemingly starting in somewhat familiar territory, he immediately diverges from the norm, challenging the conventions of his day. He addresses the wives first and as moral equals. Speaking to husbands, the parallels with traditional codes disappear as husbands are not instructed to rule, but to love and to love as they love themselves and to become one with their wives. Again, this is a call for unity and thus equality.

It is also an elimination of the subjection that was the norm for the time. As the husband and wife, become one, where is there room for subjection? At one level, this is a call to view marriage as a team of equal partners, with husband and wife as one team. I believe even this is an inadequate picture. The oneness here is something going beyond simply working as a team; it is a unity of spirit. It is the vague quality sometimes glimpsed in those who have been married for a long time and who are in such harmony it becomes difficult to picture one without the other, to see them as truly one.

Many are critical of Paul and this teaching, but what he does here, as so much of the Bibles teaching, is start with where people are, and then show them where they should be. While there is much to be critical of how women were viewed during the first century, I do not see anything to be critical of in Paul's description of where we should end up.

It is true this teaching has been misused over the years. Women have been told they must submit, as if that was the beginning and end of the teaching, forgetting about the whole "submitting to one another" thing at the start, and the much large teaching to husbands that follows. This is a problem with how this passage is used, or misused, and not with what it actually teaches.

Finally, we must remember Paul wrote to a world that had a significantly different view of women than today. In a lot of ways, it was written to a world that had not yet learned much of what this passage teaches. Given our culture has learned at least some of these lessons, we can, like Paul's reader start where we are. There is no need to go backward, but we can start where we are as we seek to achieve the goal Paul sets forth; the two can live as one.

SUGGESTIONS

What follows are some suggestions based on 45 years of marriage. They have no more to suggest them, than these are things that have worked for us. Nor is this, by any means, a complete list, but a few key things, that again have worked for us. If you do not think some of these will work in your situation feel free to adapt them, or even replace them, with what will work for you. However, if you do not think one of these will work, be sure to pray about it and ask why not? Is it because of you, or your spouse? If it is because of you, then you should pray about whether this is something you should change. Having a good marriage is tough but the rewards are tremendous, and no matter how good it gets, it can always get better.

Perhaps the most difficult aspect is since every person is unique so will every marriage. Will these improve your marriage? Maybe, maybe not, as the most important thing is to realize that marriage takes work. You should not expect to neglect your marriage and just assume all will work out well. Rather make your marriage something you work to improve and find what works for you as a couple. What follows is Elgin's comment to husbands.

Husband To Husband

We husbands are commanded to love our wives. Once you have made the choice to love your wife, then what? What does that mean on a day to day basis? First, tell her you love her, preferably daily. We guys are, as a general rule, not as expressive as women. There have been several times my wife and I have been watching a movie when two guys have some meaningful scene where they resolve some conflict or express thanks, all with a couple of words, and often with words which dance around the main issue. While now she marvels at it, earlier in our marriage she would ask, "That's it? That's all they are going to say?" or even more bluntly "Do guys really talk like that?" Yes, we do. While we may not be very verbal with other guys; we should be able to open up with our wives and tell them how we feel.

Second, show her you love her. While this could mean things like buying her flowers on special days, there are by no means any limitations. In fact, buying gifts on special days, is not something we normally do as a couple, which does not mean I do not buy my wife gifts like flowers, I do. I just do not do so only when expected. Frankly, if you are only showing her you love her on the special days, that is not enough.

29

You should constantly be looking for ways to express your love. Doing this will depend on you, her, and the moment. It could be taking her out to a nice dinner at her favorite restaurant, or simply taking out the trash. The key is always to be looking out for the little ways to make her life better and doing it because you love her.

Finally, learn to listen. Men are doers. We like to have goals to accomplish and missions to perform. We want to get things done. When we hear about a problem, our first instinct is to try and solve the problem. Early in our marriage, when my wife would share a problem, I wanted to jump in and solve it for her. It was big mistake causing a lot of needless tension in our marriage. She really wanted me to become a part of her life. She wanted to share what was going on. She did not need or want a solution.

Learn to distinguish between when your wife is seeking a solution, or just sharing. At first you may literally need to ask her, "are you sharing or seeking a solution," which does not mean you can just ignore the sharing conversations, as they are probably the most important ones. It took a lot of work, for me, to learn to listen while resisting the impulse to try and fix everything, but it has helped us to become one. In the next section my wife will address other wives.

Wife to Wife

Probably the most important thing to remember is that men and women are different, not just physically but emotionally and mentally. Growing up with my mother, my sister, and my girlfriends, I had a lot of experience talking to them. I didn't really talk to the boys back then. It wasn't until I was in college when I understood I was a woman and what that meant in a relational sense. When I got my first flat tire, I realized I could ask one of the guys to help instead of doing it myself.

Still, when I got married, I was not prepared for just how different my husband was from me. Communication with my mother, sister, and friends just seemed easier, and more fluid. We would sit down and talk it out when there was a problem, but somehow that did not seem to work the same with my husband.

Looking back now, I realize in many ways, I was expecting my husband to react to things the same way my women friends did, and when he didn't, I would get frustrated and make assumptions that were often wrong, such as he was insensitive or did not care. Usually, from there, the conversation would deteriorate into an argument. Eventually, we both learned to communicate more effectively.

One of the big things I learned was not to assume that he can read my mind. Many an argument could have been avoided if I had just been clearer about what my concerns were. As he pointed out in his section written to husbands, one example of this was whether I was seeking advice, or just wanting to share, but it was more than this. Many times, I read into in his actions things he was not actually saying or thinking.

Finally, it is important to remember that men react differently to conflict than women. Following a conflict men's brains release chemicals suppressing memory and give a sense of accomplishment. Women brains release different chemicals that heighten memory and reflection. Many times, we would be in an argument, and afterward, I would go over and over what had happened in my mind, sometimes for days. I would then go to talk to him, and he would be completely oblivious. For him, he had walked away thinking it was at least good we had aired our differences and worked things out, and then he put it behind him. This is not to say one side is the right way, but men and women approach things differently, and understanding this will help to work through these issues.

Couple to Couple

At each moment in your marriage, you as a couple are either coming closer together or drifting farther apart. This does not mean you need to do everything together and there is no time for yourself, but it does mean you should find something you both enjoy. As each of you think about the things you like to do, give higher priority to the things you have in common. Be willing to compromise on the little details and focus on the common aspects.

One thing that brings us together is playing computer games. Left to ourselves we would play different types of games, but we have been able to find games that together we can play as a team. Hanna handles the mouse, and I the keyboard. Would it be "easier" to play alone? Perhaps, but for us, when we game together, the together is more important than the game. As a result, we have spent many wonderful hours together roaming the countryside of Skyrim, which at the time of this writing is our favorite game.

It works for us. That it would not work for you is fine, you may not like computer games or even computers. The real question is what does work for you? What do you have in common you can do, which would bring you closer together? It could be hiking, building puzzles, bird-watching, or any number of things, but it should be something.

Nor is gaming the only thing we do together. As we have sought to find things that we both enjoy together, over the years, the time for ourselves has just naturally decreased to the point that now when we are doing things alone it feels like something is missing. In fact, now the main things we do alone are work-related. Your list will be unique, just as you are unique. It will take some compromise, give and take, and even some trial and error, but over time as your list of common interests grows, the two will increasingly become the one.

APPENDIX

Outline focusing on the Teaching on Marriage in 5:21-33

Opening: By the will of God (1:1-2)
Body: (1:3-6:20)
    God's Plan for the Church (1:3-3:21)
      God's Role in Salvation (1:3-23)
      Our Role in Salvation (2:1-10)
      The Church (2:11-22)
      The Secret of the Gentiles (3:1-13)
      Concluding Prayer (3:14-22)
    Application: Living God's Will (4:1-6:20)
      Living the Calling (4:1-16)
      Do Not Live Like the Gentiles (4:17-32)
      Live in Love (5:1-5:5)
      Live as Children of Light (5:6-5:14)
      Be Careful how you Live (5:15-6:9)
        Be filled with the spirit (5:15-18)
          In worshipping God (5:19-20)
          In relationship with others:
          Submitting to one another (5:21-6:9)
            Submitting one to another (5:21)
            Wives and Husbands (5:22-33)
              Wives (5:22-27)
              Husbands (5:28-33)
            Children and Parents (6:1-4)
            Slaves and Masters (6:5-9)
    The Armor of God (6:10-20)
Closing: (6:21-24)

TOPICAL LINE DRIVES

Straight to the Point in under 44 Pages

All Topical Line Drives volumes are priced at $4.99 print and 99¢ in all ebook formats.

Available

Generous Quantity Discounts Available
Dealer Inquiries Welcome
Energion Publications — P.O. Box 841
Gonzalez, FL 32560
Website: http://energionpubs.com
Phone: (850) 525-3916

ALSO FROM **ENERGION PUBLICATIONS**

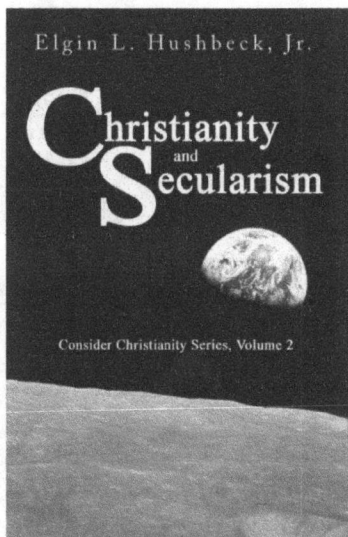

Hushbeck is truly a present day champion in defense of Christianity and the Bible.

Dr. Robert McKibben
United Methodist Pastor,
Retired

BY ELGIN HUSHBECK, JR.

Closely argued, deeply informed, highly sensitive to the issues.

Dallas Willard
Philosopher and author

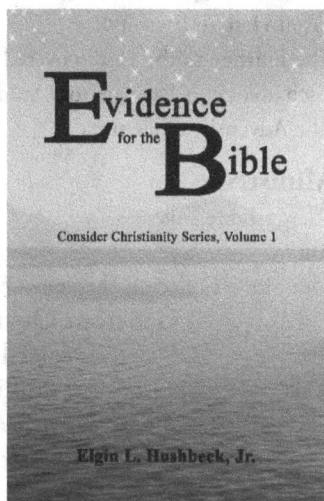

MORE FROM ENERGION PUBLICATIONS

Personal Study

Holy Smoke! Unholy Fire	Bob McKibben	$14.99
The Jesus Paradigm	David Alan Black	$17.99
When People Speak for God	Henry Neufeld	$17.99
The Sacred Journey	Chris Surber	$11.99

Christian Living

Faith in the Public Square	Robert D. Cornwall	$16.99
Grief: Finding the Candle of Light	Jody Neufeld	$8.99
Crossing the Street	Robert LaRochelle	$16.99
Life in the Spirit	J. Hamilton Weston	$12.99

Bible Study

Learning and Living Scripture	Lentz/Neufeld	$12.99
Inspiration: Hard Questions, Honest Answers	Alden Thompson	$29.99
Colossians & Philemon	Allan R. Bevere	$12.99
Ephesians: A Participatory Study Guide	Robert D. Cornwall	$9.99

Theology

Christian Archy	David Alan Black	$9.99
The Politics of Witness	Allan R. Bevere	$9.99
Ultimate Allegiance	Robert D. Cornwall	$9.99
From Here to Eternity	Bruce Epperly	$5.99
The Journey to the Undiscovered Country	William Powell Tuck	$9.99
Eschatology: A Participatory Study Guide	Edward W. H. Vick	$9.99
The Adventist's Dilemma	Edward W. H. Vick	$14.99

Ministry

Clergy Table Talk	Kent Ira Groff	$9.99
Thrive	Ruth Fletcher	$14.99
Out of the Office: A Theology of Ministry	Bob Cornwall	$9.99

Generous Quantity Discounts Available

Dealer Inquiries Welcome

Energion Publications — P.O. Box 841

Gonzalez, FL_ 32560

Website: http://energionpubs.com

Phone: (850) 525-3916

www.ingramcontent.com/pod-product-compliance
Lightning Source LLC
Chambersburg PA
CBHW011750020426
42331CB00014B/3343